Made in the USA
Coppell, TX
24 May 2021

56270358R00057